Sometimes It Takes a Mountain

A Journey in Claiming the Idols of My Addiction

Amanda Reed

ISBN 978-1-0980-6361-0 (paperback)
ISBN 978-1-0980-6362-7 (digital)

Christian Faith Publishing, Inc.
832 Park Avenue
Meadville, PA 16335
www.christianfaithpublishing.com

Printed in the United States of America

Dedicated to my husband who so patiently loves me,
and to my parents who have never stopped praying.

Introduction

Webster's Dictionary provides two definitions of the word *addiction*. The first definition is this: "a compulsive, chronic, physiological or psychological need for a habit-forming substance, behavior, or activity having harmful physical, psychological, or social effects and typically causing well-defined symptoms (such as anxiety, irritability, tremors, or nausea) upon withdrawal or abstinence: the state of being addicted." The second definition, though more subtle, indicates a similar, though not as physically detrimental, dependency: "a strong inclination to do, use, or indulge in something repeatedly."

Addiction reveals itself to us in a variety of ways. The most commonly noted addictive behaviors are those behaviors that closely associate with definition number one: drugs, alcohol, anorexia, bulimia, cutting, pornography, and sexual addictions. The second definition allows for a wider array of addictions, such as food, cell phones, social media usage, work, money, success, power, control, exercise, fitness, and more.

The struggle with addictions lies not with the definition but, rather, with the ability to admit whether or not you personally suffer from an addiction. One can say, "Oh, I am addicted to this show on Netflix!" or "I am addicted to ice cream." These types of addictive statements seem to hold no negative stigma or any devastating repercussions. However, when someone says, "I am addicted to pornography," or "I cut," or "I struggle with anorexia," an immediate reaction (usually negative) follows.

Addictions change a person's life. This may seem like a "no-brainer" statement, but those of us who have endured the consequences of our addiction can say, "I will never be the same since my addiction." Addiction is not selective. Addiction can happen to anyone. And for the Christian, addiction remains a prevalent problem.

As a Christian, I have been saved through faith in God's grace, the grace given through the free gift of His Son, Jesus, when He died on the cross to pay the penalty of my sin (Romans 6:23; Ephesians 2:8–9). I have been forgiven of my sin (I John 1:9). I am guaranteed a home in heaven when I die. I have the Holy Spirit at work in my life, helping me live to please and honor God (Romans 7:4–6). So as I began to reflect and try to heal from my addiction (anorexia and binge eating), I thought about so many other Christians I know who struggle/have struggled with addictions too. I wrestled within myself: "Why, as a child of God, would *I* struggle with addictive behaviors? How did this happen? And how can I help others who struggle too?"

I want to clearly iterate this book is by no means a "self-help" or conclusive book on "curing" anorexia or any addiction. I am by no means a counselor, therapist, or psychiatrist. Rather, this book is more accurately described as an autobiography. Each chapter focuses on how God used His Word in my life to help me realize how addiction ruled my life and how I needed His help to overcome my addictive behaviors.

I understand each person's struggle with addiction will be different. I trust the truths from God's Word and the revelation of His work in my life will encourage you to overcome whatever addictive struggle you may have. If you are a child of God, He has promised to complete the work He has begun in you (Philippians 1:6). Don't give up! Let's press on together, learning and growing, to become more like the image "of His beloved Son, in whom we have redemption, the forgiveness of [all] our sins!" (Colossians 1:14).

The Goal—"Take 1"

Sometimes it takes a mountain;
Sometimes a troubled sea;
Sometimes it takes a desert
To get ahold of me."

—"Sometimes It Takes a Mountain" by
Mark Mathes and Gloria Gaither

I have always wanted to write a book. When I was a child, books were my favorite things. I loved visiting the library. I read all the time. I dreamed about one day writing my own work or series of books that fascinated others the way certain authors' books fascinated me. I loved learning as much as I could about a lot of different things, though history and biographies were my favorite genres. I thought maybe I could write historical fiction, or maybe fiction based on the life of a Bible character or historical figure. However, I readily admit I never thought I would write a book like this. I never dreamed I would write a book about myself. About my struggles and disasters, my sins, my weaknesses. How could anyone want to read about someone who was weak or selfish or devastated? Everyone prefers the happy endings, the victorious conquerors, the heroic efforts and accomplishments.

When I was in sixth grade, our teacher read stories to us every day after lunch. I vividly remember her reading *Banner in the Sky* by James Ramsey Ullman, a story based on the true-life events of a young man who determined to climb a mountain upon which his father had died attempting to conquer its height. I listened eagerly every day, as the young man struggled through terrible weather, difficult and dangerous precipices, hunger, mental stress and anxiety, and the doubts and fears of his fellow man. I rejoiced when he finally reached the top and exulted when the young man returned to his home, sharing the amazing story of his accomplishment, so easily believed by others to be a foolish impossibility. What a fabulous ending! Such triumph and victory! A happy ending.

As I think about that story now, I realize that it fascinated and excited me not so much because it had a happy ending but because the struggles he endured to achieve the happy ending gripped my mind and heart so that I yearned for the protagonist to conquer all his obstacles and come out victorious. If James Ramsey Ullman had written this story without including the difficult and painful details, the story's ending would have not been nearly as amazing or exciting. So it is with our lives. If we cannot include the difficult and painful circumstances in our lives, how can anyone exult and rejoice when we reach the end of our lives? While I certainly do not know when the end of my life will be, I like to think that I have climbed a mountain, so to speak, in my walk with God. I climbed it and reached the top. I endured terrible weather, dangerous precipices, mental stress and anxiety, the fear of others, but I reached the top (by God's grace); and now, here at the bottom of that mountain, I wish to reveal what I learned. Why? Because I want others to know if they are climbing the same mountain, they can come down victorious. And I hope the things I share can help the journey of others to be less circuitous, less dangerous, less devastating.

Addiction is a mountain. Anorexia was my mountain. And this mountain almost destroyed me. It destroyed relationships. It destroyed my confidence. It destroyed my comfort. It destroyed everything "good" about me. But God was—and still is—good. He works all things (including my failures) for His good and glory.

This is not my story. This is God's story. God brought me to the top of that mountain. And He brought me down again.

The Story

How could I boast of anything I've ever seen or done?
How could I dare to claim as mine the vict'ries God has won?
Where would I be had God not brought me gently to this place?
I'm here to say, "I'm nothing but a sinner saved by grace."

—"Sinner Saved by Grace"
by Gloria Gaither, William J. Gaither, and
Mitch Humphries

I grew up in a wonderful family. I have attended church since I was a baby. I asked Jesus to forgive me of my sins and to be my Savior and the Lord of my life when I was twelve years old. I have been involved in church and have attended Bible college, and by anyone's outward standards, I had it all together. I was a good Christian girl. So what happened? How did my good Christian girl image "get destroyed"?

Satan realized he had lost my soul (God promises all those who come to Him for salvation, He will not cast out (John 6:37)!), so he was going to put his powers to work to make me an ineffective follower and believer of God. And he did it by attacking the very core of my belief system—knowing and understanding whose image I bore.

Was it the image of God? Or the image I wanted?

Satan knows my heart is deceitful (Jeremiah 17:9), and he capitalized on that deceit. He began to use the praise of others to deceive me and help create the image I began to believe was mine. I am a very motivated person; I love being busy and challenged. I love, even more, the success after the challenge—even if it's cleaning the bathroom! And Satan knew that.

Growing up, I never paid too much attention to what I looked like or worried about the clothes or makeup I wore (my childhood pictures can confirm this!). Gradually, though, through everyday circumstances, Satan planted seeds of deceit in my heart.

"You're maybe a bit too chubby, and that's why a guy hasn't liked you or paid attention to you."

"Look. The girls who have the nicer clothes and wear makeup are the ones getting noticed."

"Maybe if you just flirted a little instead of being so cautious about everything, you could get somewhere with what you really want."

Some comments even rendered positivity:

"Look at what you have accomplished! Everyone knows what a wonderful person you are."

"Don't listen to what other people are trying to tell you. They are just jealous of how good you are."

"Great job being noticed for your godly character. Keep it up!"

While these statements seem helpful and constructive to one's personal self-image, Satan used them to distort my thinking of who I really was, my relationship with God, and my accountability before Him and others.

Initially, I never paid too much attention to these subtle notions. I loved school, and I loved my family and was generally content with the life I had. *But* the seeds of deceit were planted. Satan was waiting for the right time to get them to grow.

I attended my first year of college and loved it. I had a beautiful group of friends. I was busy, busy, busy. Doing, doing, doing. And without really trying, I lost weight at school.

People noticed and commented on how great I looked. I began to think, *Oh, what can I do to make this better, more noticeable? How can I get everyone to see all* my *hard work?* My motivated mind began to kick into overdrive. I began to exercise obsessively and to eat sparingly. By the end of my sophomore year, I was so thin my bones were sticking out, and a fine layer of hair had developed over my emaciated face. I was royally deceived and oblivious. Friends tried to help me, question me. I ignored them.

I was skinny! For the first time I could remember, I was wearing a small, even an extra small!

Only when a friend of my mom's visited the college and saw me (and subsequently called Mom!) did my parents discover my sorry state. Mom came to school to try to help me before she had to return home, and I finished the semester.

I went home that summer, entrenched in deceit. Now I was being told I needed to gain weight. My mind and heart lurched at this idea. I had just been working so hard to lose weight! I became angry and stubbornly refused to try any of the methods my parents suggested.

Instead, I began to binge-eat, at night or when I was by myself, so no one could see me. Oh, but God saw everything. And Satan saw. And God wept, and Satan laughed.

I went back to school my junior year, spiritually floundering. My life was a mess. The deceit in my heart continued to grow. I continued binge-eating, but I was also lying and stealing to cover up my sins. The school counselor tried to help me. I put on my "good girl" face and "did" what she said, but my heart was still deceived. I was still worrying about "my image." I was worshipping what I wanted, or what I thought I wanted.

Thanks to the binge eating, I had gained back much of the weight I had lost. My mind was so mixed up. I knew I should eat. My body needed to eat. I refused to eat (much) in front of people, but then I would binge-eat on junk later. I was living a ridiculously confusing cycle.

The anorexic mind-set of my body being my possession continued to plague me. I outwardly stopped my destructive behavior. I determined to get my act together to finish school. I wanted to "move on," but how?

During my senior year, I met my now husband. I was not skinny at this point, having hung on to the weight I gained back from the binge eating. My husband and I dated long-distance, and during this time, I lost weight again. Not as drastically as before, but my lifestyle continued to demonstrate a sorely confused and destructive self-focus.

The pattern here, as you may well recognize, lies in a twisted belief system. The Bible tells us as we think or believe in our hearts, that's the way we will live (paraphrase on Proverbs 23:7). What lies in our hearts is often hidden from other people. Our true nature lies underneath the surface and, fueled by certain circumstances, reveals itself through the choices we eventually make.

In my case, I believed I was in control. My belief about God's character and how I should relate to Him became skewed. God created me; thus, it follows I should thank Him for this life and live to please Him. God loves me; thus, it follows I should love Him by doing what He instructs me to do. God grants me mercy; thus, it follows I should constantly be aware of sin and confess it before Him so as not to incur His just wrath for my disobedience. However, instead of acknowledging my necessity for God and my dependence on Him for my abilities and possessions, I believed God didn't really know what I needed or the way I should live. So I began to hide a little here, skim through my Bible reading here, check off my "prayer for the day" there. My heart believed I could worship God my way. Or I could "do the Christian things" that were convenient. I could say the right things, even "do" the right things, but eventually, the control I wanted exposed the true nature of my heart and *what I believed*.

It was all about the image. My image. My control.

Think about It:

Does any part of my story resonate in a similar chord with your life? How?

How do phrases like "follow your heart" and "believe in yourself" resonate with you? Positively or negatively? Why?

Write down three things you believe to be true about God. Then write down how you believe you should relate to those characteristics.

The Mountain Range

I faced a mountain that I'd never faced before—
That's why I'm calling on you, Lord.
I know it's been awhile, but, Lord, please hear my prayer—
I need you like I never have before.

—"Sometimes It Takes a Mountain" by
Mark Mathes and Gloria Gaither

In *Banner in the Sky*, the mountain the young man climbs bears the name the Citadel, a treacherous mountain located in the Alps of Switzerland. If you have ever taken any notice of geography, you will observe that mountains exist in ranges. The Rocky Mountains, the Grand Tetons, the Alps, the Himalayas. Each range is made up of many mountains; each mountain has a specific height. Where I live in New England, many people take on the challenge of climbing all the "4,000 footers." New England contains sixty-seven 4,000-foot mountains. This means the mountain "has an elevation of at least 4,000 feet and a minimum of 200 feet prominence" (4000footers. com, accessed January 20, 2020). Mountains bear ridges or precipices that come off them. Some of these formations remain noticeably apparent, while others are more subtle. Between the ridges exist low points called "saddles" or "passes." These connecting points join the mountains together to form the entire range. While some mountains may look like they are separate from the others, in fact, they are connected in some way by a low ridge or pass. Therefore, each mountain can be traced to a "parent" mountain, which is the most immediate higher mountain. If you see several "parent" mountains in a row, this row is called a "lineage." From this idea of "lineage," one can determine the prominence of a mountain. Basically, the prominence of a mountain is determined from the difference in elevation between the mountain's summit and the highest connecting saddle or pass to its parent (http://www.surgent.net/highpoints/prominence.html, accessed January 20, 2020). Mountains connect; each mountain, while varying in heights and depths, ridges and precipices, remains connected to all the other mountains by those "saddles" or "passes." As I reflect on my life and my struggles with addiction, I view that experience as a mountain in the range of my life. This range of "mountains" connects to the others by various "passes." When climbing a mountain, you may be provided with a map or signposts along the way, warning you or instructing you of places to avoid, trails to maintain, and outcroppings and precipices from which you should turn. So here, I want to give you a bit of a "trail map," so to speak, on the mountain of anorexia and its connection to the mountain of addiction.

I have hiked up various mountains while hunting with my husband, but I really have no idea the heights of any of those mountains. I know I relished having reached "the top" and have stood in awe at the vastness of the landscape. Reaching the top of any mountain, no matter its height, takes work. And often, it leaves you with sore muscles and blisters when you get back to the bottom. Anorexia left me with a lot of blisters and sore muscles. Climbing down was a lot easier than climbing up, though it still took work, and I had to keep going. I couldn't stop, or I would never get back home.

My mountain range most likely started with growing up, becoming a Christian, learning and growing in church. But within those mountains and passes, I began to take shortcuts. I began to ignore little warning signs on the map (Scripture) and signposts, thinking, *I have gotten this far. Why do I need to heed any of those warnings?* With anorexia, I came through this "pass" of wanting to become a certain person so others would "like me." This pass started with subtle twists and turns easing up into a dizzying mountain height I never could have anticipated. Anorexia started with replacing God with my own image. I believed I could get what I wanted (acceptance from others) by establishing my own system of "godly" living. Essentially, I acknowledged God was with me and part of my life, but I really did not need Him to help me. I had it all together, and I did not need all the "things" He said I needed. Like accountability. Like listening to counsel and heeding the warnings people were begging me to see. Like admitting my lifestyle was a direct violation of the very character of God, the God I declared to know.

In the first few chapters of Genesis, we read how God created man in *His image*. Everything was perfect, beautiful, good. God gave Adam and Eve one minor instruction: they were not to eat of the tree of the knowledge of good and evil. That's it. Everything else was at their disposal. Communication with God was not hindered. They could go anywhere in the Garden of Eden, do anything, care for everything—no work, no sweat, no anxiety. A perfect life. But then, Adam and Eve chose to believe what they wanted instead of what God expressly told them. They worshipped another god. They worshipped their own sense of belief, their own desire for control. And mankind was doomed to sin and death for eternity. All because of a deceived belief system. This deceived belief system is sin. Sin is anything that displeases or denounces the character of God. Sin exalts people, things, personalities, possessions over the person of God; therefore, when we sin, our lives contradict God. Contradicting God results in consequences. Anytime we reject or ignore the rules of an authority, we must be prepared to suffer the consequences.

Many years after Adam and Eve's first sin, God gave the Ten Commandments to Moses. In these commandments, God made it very clear His people were not to worship any other god, nor were they to make anything like a god, nothing that would cause them to worship anything other than *Him*. He alone was to be worshipped (Exodus 20:1–6). But the entire Old Testament is replete with story after story of the sorry tale of God's chosen people, the Israelites, falling away from God into idolatry, worshipping other things/gods, rather than God alone.

The command God gave them (and to us!) was so simple. "You shall have no other gods before me. You shall not make for yourself a carved image, or any likeness of anything that is in the heaven above, or that is in the earth beneath, or that is in the water under the earth. You shall not bow down to them or serve them" (Exodus 20: 3–4a ESV). I ignored this signpost. I declared I would not worship anything else. But oh, how like the Israelites I was! How idolatrous was my heart! And anorexia was just one part of that idolatrous lifestyle.

Anorexia pushed my image above the image of God. Therefore, I was willing to do whatever it took to be skinny. Whether it was exercising like a crazy person or eating like a bird—a very tiny bird, mind you. Satan is a master at getting us to believe our idol worship is *not* a sin. I was so deceived I actually believed I was glorifying God by "being healthy." After all, lots of Biblical counselors and medical advice on losing weight and being fit and healthy promoted exercise and eating small portions. So I was doing it "the right way." I was climbing the right trail. I would not turn back or retrace my steps. I was confident this was where I wanted and needed to go.

Addictive behavior works to promote our own images above the image of God. My anorexic struggles were a sin. I ignored the signpost of idol worship and walked down the trail of "my control." Like Adam and Eve, I saw something I thought was good. Losing weight and eating healthy and exercising are all good things. But instead of allowing God and His Word to guide my mountain trek, I replaced His map with my own and followed the trails I thought were best.

Scripture tells us our hearts are deceitful above all things and desperately sick (Jeremiah 17:9). Watch out for your heart; it will erect idols you cannot bear to have in your life. So as much as this world tells you to follow your dreams or your heart, *don't do it*. Don't follow that trail. I did it. And I was very nearly destroyed.

Think about It:

What kind of image do you want? Does this image reflect the character of God? Why or why not?

What areas of your life do you have the most control (work, home, your body, your phone, etc.)? How can this control become an idol in your life?

What kinds of things do you enjoy? These "enjoyable" things can become idols. In what ways are you worshipping those things instead of worshipping God?

How have you allowed these "good things" to dominate your life? Do you think you are addicted to any of them? Why or why not?

Let's Try This Trail

Forgive me, Jesus; I thought I could control
Whatever life would throw my way.
But this, I will admit, has brought me to my knees.
I need you, Lord, and I'm not ashamed to say,
"Sometimes it takes a mountain…"

—"Sometimes It Takes a Mountain" by
Mark Mathes and Gloria Gaither

Certainly, having climbed any mountain allows for some bit of pride in that accomplishment. People regularly post pictures from the top of any given "hike," relating their heightened achievement. Have you ever been told to "take pride in your work or your accomplishments" or "be proud of who you are"? These statements float around a lot—whether it's a celebrity talking about their latest achievements or a blogger touting their newest recipe or method for creativity. "Taking pride" in what we have done is easy. But is it right?

I mentioned the first signpost in the mountain of anorexia as "idols," marking the trail of "my control." As you continue past that signpost, you find you come to the signpost of "pride." This signpost resonates with your heart because the images on it look a lot like the image you desperately try to "find." Pride tells you all the things you want to hear and rarely tells you if you are wrong. Pride exalts your actions and words above the actions and words of others, including God. It's another step down the trail of control.

An anorexic person begins to believe she is doing everything right by her body. She deprives herself of necessary food and will exercise to maintain a certain look or weight. She will have panic attacks at the thought of going out to eat with family or friends because she does not want to eat in front of them—she *can't* eat in front of them—and eating will destroy the image she is creating. Her mind will wrestle with thoughts about what is the healthiest thing to eat. She will obsessively read health blogs and weight loss articles, trying to find the best method for her weight loss journey. She will refuse any method that requires her to be accountable to someone about eating, because, obviously (she thinks), eating is what made her "fat" or "unattractive." Eating makes her gain weight, and gaining weight is not good for her! She will starve herself, eating only very small amounts of food, refusing food offered to her by others, and limiting her intake of "unhealthy" things, such as sweets, bread, and so on. She will cling to every sort of praise or comment about her looks. Her image is everything to her. Her hard work at being thin and attractive makes her proud. Look at what she has accomplished!

What *has* she accomplished? In my life, I did all these things. I thought I had accomplished what I wanted—even what other people wanted for me. Hadn't they said I looked good when I lost weight? Now, they were saying I needed to gain weight? I gained nothing—nothing but destroyed relationships, a confused body, and a twisted mind. I lost so many dear friends; the ability to communicate with them seemed destroyed (many of these friends tried to help, but in my pride, I would not listen). My parents and family were so confused and hurt with how I was treating them and myself. I would not tell anyone what I was thinking, because, honestly, I did not know what to think anymore. Inwardly, I knew I needed help. How I was living was wrong, but how could I fix it? I was losing control of the "good life" I had. What happened? I began to walk faster along the trail, climbing up, trying to find a glimpse of the top and what I wanted, but getting nowhere.

I will emphatically declare, "I am a *proud person!*" Anorexia revealed this in my life. Refusing to listen to counsel revealed this in my life. Hiding things from others revealed how I thought about myself and others. Pride is a sin.

I came to realize this more fully when I had children, when my relationship with my husband was strained, when I could not talk to my parents or have them visit me without feeling frustrated with myself, when I wanted friendships but didn't know where to begin or what to say.

Reading my Bible revealed to me my desire for control, how my desire for the image I wanted and my roller-coaster lifestyle stemmed from a proud heart. The book of Proverbs helped me understand how foolish I was to live this way, how my control could not be—and was not—possible. I had not taken the time to "ponder the path of my feet" (Proverbs 4:26); instead, I followed my own heart (which is prone to foolishness), and my "ways [began to] wander, and [I did] not know it" (Proverbs 5:6).

Further, reading the books of the prophets revealed how like the Israelites I was—doing what I wanted and worshipping what I wanted and the way I wanted. Proudly exalting my image above the image of God. And it was destroying me—much like the way the Israelites were constantly being taken captive and held in bondage. In the book of Jeremiah, God constantly implores the Israelites to return to following Him and His ways. Jeremiah, the prophet, declares God's words of hope and promise, giving them an example of being a clay pot in the potter's hands, being molded and shaped into something good. God declares, "O house of Israel, can I not do with you as this potter has done?... Behold, like the clay in the potter's hand, so are you in my hand, O house of Israel... Return, every one from his evil way, and amend your evil ways and your evil deeds" (Jeremiah 18:6, 11b). God warns them disaster will come to them if they continue to ignore His warnings and pleas for repentance. Sadly, Jeremiah writes, "But they say... 'We will follow our own plans, and will every one act according to the stubbornness of his evil heart'" (Jeremiah 18:12). And God had to punish them "because they have stiffened their neck, refusing to hear my words" (Jeremiah 19:15b).

Addictions of all kinds reveal the intent of your heart to promote what you want over what God wants. Addiction stems from a heart determined to have the image you want. In anorexia, it starts with wanting to be thin or healthy. In social media, it starts with wanting to be connected and noticed by other people. In drugs or alcohol, it starts with wanting to fit in or ease a painful area of your life. In work, it starts with wanting to be successful or make enough money to provide for your family. In eating, it starts with just being hungry. In pornography, it starts with being curious or having a sexual desire. But the addiction grows, and the trail gets more treacherous when pride at what you have done or how you are accepted by others or having what you believe you "deserve" begins to push God even farther out of the picture. And you begin to be taken captive by that "thing." Your mind and heart are held in bondage, and soon, all your actions, thoughts, and words are consumed with that obsession. You become selfish, wanting only that "thing" (e.g., being thin or exercising, wanting that drug or alcohol, needing to be on that social media, having to be at work or think about work or making money, feeling hungry or the need to be satisfied with food, needing to see that pornographic site "one more time").

In my case, anorexia started with just wanting to lose some extra weight and be fit like other people. To look good for other people, to have people say I was pretty or attractive. Initially, not a bad thing, but it became a sin when I took God out of the picture (remember that first signpost?) and placed my emaciated, confused, exercise-obsessed body on the altar of my heart and mind. The pride of my heart consumed me. And it will consume you.

Think about It:

What everyday things make you happy? Why do these things make you happy?

What is your motivation every day? Why is this your motivation?

How has this motivating "thing" become an obsession in your life?

Do you think you "have it all together"? Why? Do you see this as prideful? Why or why not?

Do you communicate well with other people? Do other people enjoy talking to you?

If you answered no, you need to ask yourself, "Why?" If others do not enjoy talking to you or being with you, is there only one thing you focus on all the time? Do you scoff at people who are different from you? Do you selfishly make or have time for just "what you want"?

Ask God to reveal areas of pride in your life. Write them down here:

Well, This Trail Looks Fine

I'm fine; yeah, I'm fine; oh, I'm fine; hey, I'm fine, but I'm not—
I'm broken.
And when it's out of control, I say it's under control, but it's not—
And you know it.
I don't know why it's so hard to admit it
When being honest is the only way to fix it.
There's no failure, no fall;
There's no sin you don't already know,
So let the truth be told.

—"Truth Be Told" by Matthew West

I realized, fairly quickly, that anorexia was destroying my life (hence, my determination to finish school and move on with life.) However, I could not let go of the idol worship and pride. I had walked past those signposts and was still stumbling my way down that path of "control." I had worked so hard. Why was this not working out the way I thought it would? Why was I not happy? Why had I hurt so many people and destroyed so many relationships? Why did God seem so far away?

All these questions—and more—swirled around in my mind and heart. And soon, I found myself at another signpost. This signpost led me farther down the trail, continuing to deceive me and tell me it was "all God's fault" for making me become anorexic. My situation was the fault of "everyone else" because "no one else understood what I was going through"; no one else "admitted they had a problem with this, so obviously, their counsel is irrelevant." I was a "good person," a Christian! Surely, I could just brush it all under the rug and be "fine." I could just ignore what other people were telling me—they had no clue. After all, it was their fault—if they had just left me alone and not said anything about me being "fat" or "big" or "eating too much," which then led to "wanting to be healthy" and losing weight and exercising "like I was supposed to," then I would not be in this mess. I should blame them. It was all their fault.

I began believing all these things. And this next signpost revealed itself as "anger." Anger at other people. Anger at God. Anger at myself.

Anger reveals itself in an anorexic person in the way they speak/respond to others. A friend or family member may express concern, but an anorexic person responds with a sharp retort to the effect of "You just don't understand!" Or they may bottle the anger inside and stubbornly refuse to speak about their problems. I can say I responded in both ways. "A fool gives full vent to his spirit... Do you see a man who is hasty in his words? There is more hope for a fool than for him... A man of wrath stirs up strife, and one given to anger causes much transgression" (Proverbs 29: 11a, 20, 22).

Angry people also play the "blame game." Instead of admitting areas of sin, a person controlled by their addiction will respond by angrily blaming other people for their problems. Excuses, accusations, and even lies often become a regular part of their conversations. They will not listen to the concerns or counsel of others; instead, they will declare that other people are the ones with the problems! Addicted people often cannot or will not see that their problems are their own. Anger blinds them and causes them to see only the "problems" of other people.

In the book of Hosea, God describes how the people of Israel have rejected God's ways. He uses the living example of the prophet Hosea to illustrate the sin of Israel. Hosea receives an instruction from God to marry a prostitute named Gomer. Each time she (Gomer) returns to her sinful, unfaithful lifestyle, God instructs Hosea to buy her back. God explains the people of Israel are like that prostitute—they reject their husband (God) for the pleasures of sin. They remain unrepentant, rejecting God's love. God declares, "When I would heal Israel, the iniquity of Ephraim is revealed, and the evil deeds of Samaria; for they deal falsely…they do not consider that I remember all their evil. Now their deeds surround them; they are before my face… For with hearts like an oven they approach their intrigue; all night their anger smolders; in the morning it blazes like a flaming fire… The pride of Israel testifies to his face; yet they do not return to the LORD their God, nor seek Him, for all this…they rebel against me…they devise evil against me…because of the insolence of their tongue. This shall be their derision" (Hosea 7:1–2, 6, 10, 14–16).

Anger destroys your ability to see yourself and your situations clearly. As described in Hosea, the Israelites were so consumed with their sin and their desire for other things, they were completely oblivious to their own destruction. They spoke and thought evil of the only One who had been faithful to them. They rejected the very One who loved them unconditionally. Addiction and anger work hand in hand to destroy you.

Anger is another signpost on that terrible trail of "control." Anger makes the trail even more treacherous. Anger confirms you don't need to go back and start over at the bottom of the mountain. Anger looks around and says, "You are fine." And if someone comes along the trail trying to bring you back down or offer you help, you refuse. Satan loves this. It's further revelation that God no longer has a place in your life. It's proof you are worshipping yourself. How? Because God clearly states a person who is wise will listen to counsel (Proverbs 9:9). A person who depends on God will not be easily angered, but will listen instead (James 1:19–20). A person who receives counsel from another person will not reject that counsel, but will ask for help and admit his sin (Proverbs 12:15; Proverbs 14:14–17). Anger is a sin.

And the mountain is becoming harder and harder to climb.

Think about It:

Do you easily become angry?

What things or people make you angry? Why?

Do you quickly justify your anger? Why?

How does the verse "Let every person be swift to hear, slow to speak, and slow to anger" resonate in your life? Do you find yourself always being the first to speak when confronted, or do you listen?

Ask God to reveal to you the areas of your life that make you angry. Write them here:

Sidetracked

O to grace, how great a debtor
Daily I'm constrained to be.
Let Thy goodness, like a fetter,
Bind my wand'ring heart to Thee.
Prone to wander, Lord, I feel it;
Prone to leave the God I love!

—"Come Thou Fount" by Robert Robinson

If you are struggling with a particular addiction, you will readily admit to making lots of excuses for "why" you are indulging that addiction. These excuses often run in circles. You blame past circumstances, people, or events for making you succumb to your particular addiction. I was no different.

I blamed being "fat" on not being educated about healthy "stuff." I blamed it on my mom's diabetes and the changes she was having to make health-wise, so clearly, I needed to do that too so I wouldn't become diabetic. I blamed it on other people saying negative things about me (their choice—but my response was to be judgmental back). I blamed it on God for making me so confused (He cannot confuse me; He is God!).

So many reasons and so many excuses. But when I look at the situation now, I recognize I have no one to blame but myself. I made a choice. And choices happened (and continue to happen!) every day. As I reflect on "how I became anorexic," I realize that choice became a product of thousands of other "choices." Choices about what to think, what to say, excuses to make, sins to leave unconfessed, the Holy Spirit to ignore.

I realized many of my past choices were sinful. I outwardly looked and said all the right, godly, obedient things; but inwardly, I was selfish, judgmental, jealous, bitter—the list could go on and on. The Holy Spirit would convict me of something, but instead of confessing that sin immediately, I hung on to it, locking it away for later.

Mountain trails are often circuitous. And so is the trail of addiction. Whatever your addictive struggle, as you reflect on past events, you will realize places and moments where you became sidetracked. Instead of pulling out the right map (the Bible), you saw a trail that "looked good" and followed that one instead; and then you found another, and another, and another. And before you realized it, the trails were so tangled, you couldn't even remember where the journey exactly began. You just knew it was not getting you where you thought you were going.

In today's information-loaded world, we are distracted by so many things. News, social media, information about any subject we can think of are readily available to us. With just a few taps or clicks, we can find information about anything. These side trails distract us and lure us farther and farther down the trail of our controlling addiction. Whether you seek information about health and fitness, money, food, or success, the wide world of the Web will gladly offer you all kinds of trails to take. And the addiction becomes harder and harder to distinguish. The trails become harder to see, and truth becomes harder to determine. Even if you do have limited screen times, our hearts and minds conjure up all kinds of information to easily deceive and distract us.

Addictions are not a "new thing." Addictions have plagued people for generations. You may not even be addicted to any type of website or social media. Instead, your addiction could be a direct product of your mind and heart. Satan can so easily deceive you just by using your thoughts. In the book of Hebrews, the writer warns, "Take care, brothers, lest there be in any of you an evil, unbelieving heart, leading you to fall away from the living God" (Hebrews 3:12). What you think may be a good thing can actually be a distraction from the truth found in Christ. In chapter 5 of Hebrews, the writer further elaborates that believers must be constantly filling their minds and hearts with the "solid food" of the Word of God in order to have the "powers of discernment trained by constant practice to distinguish good from evil" (verse 14).

Your everyday choices and how you are choosing to fill your mind and heart will determine your life's trails. Allowing Satan to fill your mind with deception about people, things, possessions, status, God, your expectations, success, money (the list could go on and on) will keep you from determining what is good. You will lose your ability to discern truth from error. I did this. I allowed Satan to deceive me. I made excuses. I did not confess sin. Instead of being aware of the areas where I was susceptible to the attacks of Satan (my mind and heart), I thought that "I had it all together" and that my desires and affections were "no big deal."

The "control trail" I thought was good became a journey I could have never imagined. A trek so winding and treacherous, I could not fathom how I would ever get down. The mountain seemed higher than I ever anticipated.

Think about It:

What areas of your past still haunt you? Things people said, circumstances that "define" you, and so on. Write them down here:

How did those circumstances get you to where you are now?

How do you regularly feed and fill your mind?

Do you fill your mind with excuses and judgments of other people? How and why?

Do you feel that your life is hopeless, that you'll just be this way forever? Or do you make the excuse that "this is just the way I am"? Why?

Help!

———⁕⁘⁘⁘⁕———

I've wandered far away from God;
Now I'm coming home.
The paths of sin too long I've trod;
Lord, I'm coming home."
Coming home, coming home,
Nevermore to roam;
Open wide Thine arms of love;
Lord, I'm coming home.

—"Lord, I'm Coming Home"
by William J. Kirkpatrick

When climbing mountains, certain elevations inhibit your ability to breathe. The lack of oxygen constricts your lungs and causes dizziness, nausea, and a whole host of other repercussions. At this point, a mountain climber will admit they need help, or they won't make it back down the mountain. Breathing gives life; without breath, the ability of the brain and the heart to function will cease. And death follows.

I got to this point on the mountain. I was struggling to breathe. I needed help.

I had given birth to my second son. I knew I needed help to be a mom. I knew my marriage needed help. I knew I was floundering to keep everything "together." To maintain "the image." To stay "in control."

Desperate, I opened my Bible, which, sadly, had been dormant for a while. I started in Psalms, then Proverbs, then the major and minor prophets. And in those books, I found how dreadfully like the Israelites I was. Betraying the goodness and love of my God for the few pleasures of doing things "my way." The pride of my heart had so utterly and devastatingly deceived me. I was worshipping the idols of pride, of selfishness, of anger, and of jealousy. I finally realized I was on the totally wrong trail.

I realized my struggles with anorexia was an offshoot of the trail of control. I was proud—I wanted to look a certain way. I was selfish—no one was going to tell me what to do or how I should live. I was angry—no one would tell me there was help or how I could ask for help. I was jealous—why did I have to struggle like this? I knew I could no longer make excuses or blame someone else for giving me wrong directions. I could no longer stay on this trail, because if I did, I would never get off this mountain.

I ran to God, begging for His forgiveness, begging for Him to restore our relationship, confessing how I was living to please only myself. And I found *help*. "I lift my eyes unto the hills from whence comes my help—my help comes from the LORD!" (Psalm 121:1–2).

The hard part in this, for me, was realizing how my anorexia had started with small measures of deceit, bits of pride, sprinklings of anger and jealousy—all building up in a deceived mind, which eventually rejected the very nature and person of God (those circuitous little side trails). And I was a Christian. How did this happen? How did I so easily slip from following God (I thought) to being entrenched in an addictive behavior? My conclusion to this came through much prayer and reading of God's Word. I have concluded that, in my own life, my addictive behavior came when I chose to ignore everyday sin in my life. Gradually, my heart became calloused to the terrible attitudes, the prideful thoughts, the critical spirit, the stubborn pride, the self-exaltation; and I firmly believed I was "fine." Being "fine" was a prime stomping ground for Satan to take over my life. Dear believer, if you are not daily confessing sin (you sin every day!), you are setting yourself up for spiritual failure. I know. I have done it. I have failed. I could elaborate for pages on the deceitfulness of sin in our lives (this may be a subject matter for another book), so let me implore you to search your heart. When you admit the pride and idols of your heart fueling your addictive behavior and then ask God to help you, be prepared to be attacked *more* by Satan. Be prepared to confess to God sins of anger—anger at God allowing you to go through your particular addiction. Sins of jealousy—jealousy at how everyone else seems to have it all "together". Sins of bitter thoughts and a critical spirit. Sins of ridiculing others to make yourself look good. Ignoring these sins in your life (every day) will cause further depression, further anger, further pride, continued control.

Please do not be discouraged in this. I can tell you—I have encountered each of these struggles (and more!). God loves you, and He promises to forgive you. He promises to love you. He promises that no struggle you endure is greater than you—with *His* help.

Previously, I shared about Hosea and his prostitute wife, Gomer, and their parallel to God and the children of Israel. In that book, Hosea implores the people of Israel, "So you, by the help of your God, return, hold fast to love and justice, and wait continually for your God… Return, O Israel, to the LORD your God, for you have stumbled because of your iniquity. Take with you words and return to the LORD" (12:6, 14:1). And God promises, "I will heal their apostasy; I will love them freely" (14:4). And wonderfully, God's promises to the Israelites are the same for you and me. When you and I return to the Lord, He promises to heal us. Why do you wait, dear brother or sister? Return to the *Lord*!

Perhaps you are reading this book, and you have never made the decision to follow Jesus as your Savior. This step is crucial. You cannot defeat sin and death on your own. The Bible tells us everyone is a sinner (Romans 6:23); no one person can ever do enough good things to appease God's righteous rules and enter heaven. God has made Himself clearly known to us; we are the ones who reject Him (Romans 1:19–21). However, God promises anyone who comes to Him in repentance, declaring his or her need for mercy and asking for salvation from sin and death, He will abundantly forgive and pardon (Isaiah 55:6–7). Placing your trust in the finished work of Jesus on the cross for your sin and believing in His resurrection and intercession for you (because of His great love) will be the greatest decision of your life (1 John 4:9–15). You cannot ensure your eternal destiny without faith (Hebrews 11:6). "Believe on the Lord Jesus, and you will be saved" (Acts 16:31)! Don't wait! Trust Him *now*!

It's time to get off the mountain. Let's go home.

Note: If you are reading this book to seek ways to help another individual in the throes of addiction, please know you *cannot* change that person. You cannot get them to "radically change." Any person who struggles with addictive behavior must come to this conclusion on their own. This person must seek help of his or her own volition. So pray. Pray God will soften her heart to understand her sin. Pray God will reveal his pride and anger so he will return to God. Pray, pray, pray. In trying to help an addicted person, prayer remains the best method of help.

In addition to prayer, seek for ways to help this person. The addicted person will probably respond negatively to your help. Do not be discouraged. Ask God to show you ways you can be a help to them, ways you can unobtrusively show the love of God. Anger and demands of "change" will only add fuel to an already-roaring fire of idolatry—in the addicted person's heart and in your heart.

Think about It:

What is your addiction? How do you know this?

Are you willing to admit you need help? Why or why not?

If you have not accepted Christ as your Savior, what is holding you back? Why do you find it hard to take this step?

What Now?

I run to Christ when stalked by sin
And find a sure escape.
"Deliver me," I cry to Him;
Temptation yields to grace.
I run to Christ when plagued by shame
And find my one defense.
"I bore God's wrath," He pleads my case—
My Advocate and Friend.

—"I Run to Christ"
by Chris Anderson

So I took the wrong trail. I knew that. But then I found myself asking, "What now?" I admitted I had a problem, asked God to forgive me, but now what? Where and how was I going to get the spiritual and mental help I so desperately wanted and needed? I knew I did not want to keep struggling every day like this. Struggling to promote my image of having it all together, but knowing *I did not* have it all together. I did not want my children and my husband to be living with an emotional basket case every day. This was not right. I knew God did not intend for this to be my life. So how could I get help? How could I really give up the control I had been holding on to for so long?

Do you have these same thoughts? Do you struggle to admit you need help? Do you want help but don't know whom to ask? Unfortunately, as a Christian, I felt so much guilt in admitting I had a sin problem. I was supposed to have it all together, right? I was not supposed to struggle like this, right? Why had no one come to me and said, "I see you are struggling with anorexia. I have too. Let me help you." (The counselor at school had tried to help me, but I felt like she couldn't *really* understand my struggles. This was an evidence I still wanted to maintain my control—something I didn't fully grasp until now.)

And here again, I went to the only place I knew could comfort me: *the Word of God*, my Bible.

In His Word, I found strength and comfort. In my restored relationship with Him, I found hope and wisdom. You can find it too. If you are struggling with an addiction, please know I have struggled too. The help I found did not come from a step-by-step recovery plan or through some man-made methodology. No. My help came from the pages of my Bible. My help came when I went to the throne room of God and begged for His mercy. My help came when I *admitted* I needed help, and God richly supplied (and supplies every day) His wisdom when I *humbly asked*.

God's Word contains all the answers for your confusion. Talking to Him (prayer) grants you the ability to gain true wisdom. You must accept, by faith, that God's ways are best. You *must* give up the control you have had for so long. It's hard. Admitting failure stinks. Admitting sin hurts. But oh, how much richer and sweeter will be your relationship with God—and with others. How great to reconsider the love He has for *you*. How refreshing to go to Him and find greater peace and satisfaction than your addictive behaviors could ever give you.

"In the fear of the Lord is a fountain of life, that one may turn from the snares of death" (Proverbs 14:27). Get off that trail. Back away from those snares. Pull out that trail map, which is probably down at the very bottom of your life's "backpack." Read it, study it, and never let it go.

Think about It:

Do you read your Bible? How often?

What is your motivation for reading your Bible?

What sins do you struggle with every day? List them here:

Do you really think or believe God can help you overcome these sins? Why or why not?

Getting Down the Mountain

When the valley is deep; when the mountain is steep;
When the body is weary; when we stumble and fall;
When the choices are hard; when we're battered and scarred;
When we've spent our resources; when we've given our all—
In Jesus' name we press on! In Jesus' name we press on!
Dear Lord, with the prize clear before our eyes—
We find the strength
To press on!

—"Press On"
by Daniel L. Burgess/Selah

So now comes the partially relieving part, but also the part where panic can set in. You're coming down the mountain, but there are still a lot of what-ifs. "What if" I take the wrong trail again? How will I know what is the right way down? "What if" the map is wrong? Many mountain climbers play the mind game, particularly when their minds have been clouded by the things they have endured. And life is no different.

Much of what we say and do is a direct reflection of how we think. At the core of an addictive behavior is a mind that thinks the wrong things. Thoughts permeate us every second of every day. We are constantly thinking. In anorexia, we think, *How can I stay skinny? How can I look good to others? How can I avoid eating in front of others, thus destroying my image? When can I sneak away to exercise more?* The list could go on and on. This thinking is flawed; it is (as mentioned previously) selfish and prideful. Did you notice all the "I"s? Clearly, this mind is thinking on only one thing: self—*myself.*

Therefore, when you have recognized your need for God and have admitted your sins of pride and control, you *must* change your thinking. Otherwise, you will continue to think and do all the same things. Every day. All over again. So what next? How do I change a thinking that is so entrenched in deceit?

I am glad you asked, because I asked myself the very same thing. And it should come as no surprise to you now at this point in the book: I changed my thinking by focusing on different things. I no longer focused on myself; I focused on God. I no longer read health articles; I read my Bible. I no longer tried to hide my eating; I began eating with my children, with my family. I am not saying this was easy. It was (is) not easy.

For some reason, I found I struggled most when I was around people who loved me—people who were with me during my anorexia, mainly my family. So I struggle most when I go to my parents' house, when I go out to eat with them or have to make food choices in front of them. My mind freezes. Satan begins firing deceitful arrows into my mind of how my parents must be so ashamed or how my family is watching my every move to make sure I'm not crazy again. And then, I get angry.

This journey of renewing my mind in the things of God is not easy. I have been (am) discovering this more every day. I cannot—*I must not*—quit. I cannot bear to deny my Savior again. I cannot bear to be filled with pride again. I cannot bear to sideline myself in the race to heaven. I must stay focused. *I must renew my mind* (Ephesians 4:23).

The book of Philippians contains wonderful insight on the trek of the Christian. The Apostle Paul instructs the believers to "only let your manner of life be worthy of the Gospel of Christ" (1:27). So how were they (and we) supposed to do this? Paul continues instructing them about how they should think like Christ, act like Christ, speak like Christ. He tells them how he considers his life to be nothing unless he can "know" Christ (3:8–10). Paul then reminds them he has certainly not attained full knowledge of Christ, but he determines to "press on" to make that his life's goal (3:12). He declares he will forget the things of his past and "strain forward" to the "prize of the upward call of God in Christ Jesus" (3:13–14). So how, as a Christian, can I keep "pressing on"? Paul answers that in chapter 4 and verse 8: "Finally, brothers, whatever is true, whatever is honorable, whatever is just, whatever is pure, whatever is lovely, whatever is commendable, if there is any excellence, if there is anything worthy of praise, think about these things." And in order to find those things, I must look to the only true source of *truth*: the Word of God.

Therefore, I know I need to keep reading my Bible. I need to listen to *truth*. Instead of listening to health podcasts or reading weight loss articles, I will listen to sermons and read devotionals. I will read my Bible. I will pray. When Satan begins filling my mind with depression, I will run to God. I will cry out to Him for help. I will ask someone to pray for me. And here's the hardest part: *I will admit I need help.*

For some reason, I am so bent on not admitting failure, on not asking for help or wanting help (okay, not for "some reason"; it's the pride of my heart!). Perhaps you are this way also? Do you cringe at admitting you struggle with food or body image or pornography? Do you feel sick at the thought of admitting you are wrong? Do you become angry when someone confronts you about your disrespectful attitude or your critical and angry words? Admitting sin is hard. It feels embarrassing. Oh, but, dear believer, admitting your sin leads to a greater recognition of God. Admitting your need for help leads to a dependence on God, which cannot be replaced with material possessions or position.

Renew your mind. Change your thinking. Instead of thinking about how you can be your version of successful (thin, popular, wealthy, etc.), think on Christ. Think about His love for you; think about His dying for you—for the very sin you don't want to give up. Think about His anger at your rejection of Him; think about His mercy in granting you forgiveness. Think about His grace in giving you "second chances"; think about seeing His face one day. Think about either being called "faithful" or being a failure for the kingdom of God.

Find verses on pride, on sin, on anger, on jealousy—read the major and minor prophets, and ask God to show you where and how you need to change your thinking. Read the Epistles. Read Romans. Read *your Bible*!

Write down verses—put them where you can easily see and read them. Memorize and know His Word.

When a situation comes that is especially hard for you mentally and emotionally in relation to your addiction (for me, when I see or visit family), admit your struggle. Ask God to help you reject the deceit and make choices that please Him. This takes time. This takes purposeful prayer.

Even during my years of anorexia, pride, control, I was reading my Bible (occasionally) and going to church. The problem, however, was that my Bible reading was more like a "checklist" instead of the "life blood" of my everyday choices. So I would read my Bible, go to church, and check it off the list. Reading your Bible is not a daily "checklist." It must not be a simple task. You must take the time to study it. To ask God to reveal His truth for you and your life. Not how so-and-so should apply it, but how *you* should apply it. You should not have a ho-hum or humdrum attitude toward the truth of God. His Word must be your "go-to" for wisdom and guidance. This is where I failed. Satan so deceived me that even my Bible reading became a source of pride. In Hebrews, chapter 4, God warns us to be aware of the hardening of our hearts against Him and falling into disobedience. The sure help for this is to see His truth correctly: "For the word of God is living and active, sharper than any two-edged sword, piercing to the division of soul and spirit, of joints and marrow, and discerning the thoughts and intentions of the heart. And no creature is hidden from his sight, but all are naked and exposed to the eyes of him to whom we must give account" (Hebrews 4:12–13). So even when you think you already "know" what you are supposed to do, God's Word will reveal the areas you don't know, the sins you are trying to hide, and the ways you are "in control." God continues to carve away at those prideful and angry parts of my heart by using His Word. Don't stop reading the *right* map!

Think about It:

What situations are difficult for you to encounter in relation to your addiction (maybe being with certain people or going to a certain place)?

How can you respond biblically in this situation?

Are you motivated to overcome your addiction? Why?

What will you use as your method of overcoming addiction? How will this help you?

Do you have a trusted fellow believer who can help you be accountable in reading your Bible and praying? Write that person's name here, and determine to ask them to keep you accountable in your daily walk with God.

Facing the Crowds

Now Lord I would be Yours alone
And live so all might see
The strength to follow Your commands
Could never come from me.
Oh, Father use my ransomed life
In any way you choose;
And let my song forever be—
"My only boast is You!"

—"All I Have Is Christ"
by Bob Kauflin

The previous chapter discussed focusing our thoughts on the Word of God. However, if you are anything like me, you will struggle with admitting your failures and then having people say, "I thought you changed." Or maybe doubts will fill your mind about how people will perceive you when you admit your sins.

In *Banner in the Sky*, young Rudy comes off the mountain a different person than when he started his journey. And we are no different. Climbing the mountain of addiction will leave you a different person. You will not think the same way you thought before this trek. Ever.

I can even tell, now, if someone I am talking to or interacting with has the same struggles I do. I can tell in the worried looks at food or the avoidance of food. I can tell in the way they talk about themselves or their bodies. I can perceive a different addictive struggle by noticing how a person talks to me (or avoids talking to me) or by a person's admissions about "how they don't have a problem."

I will not be the same person I was in high school. Or in college. Or two years ago. And that's not a bad thing! I praise God for the change He has wrought in my life. In my thinking. In my desires. But this change could never have come if I had not admitted my struggles. So as I mentioned previously, *you must admit* when you have a problem; whatever your addictive struggle, you must own it and ask for help, or you will never get down the mountain. And in that admission, you will come off that mountain a totally different person.

I have more knowledge, more awareness, more discernment. I am keeping my eyes focused for those dangerous side trails I wandered on for so long. I am avoiding the "control trail." I am constantly looking at the right map (my Bible). And as I have come down the mountain and am facing a whole new expectation of others, I find I cannot go back and "redo" that mountain. I don't want to. And I won't.

So to others who have not climbed an addiction mountain, know that your loved one or friend will not ever be the same person you knew as a child, as a college roommate, as a friend. However, by God's grace, they *can* become better, wiser, stronger in their walk with God. Better at facing temptations. Wiser about the reality of sin and Satan. Stronger in the Word of God. Don't expect this change or admission to happen immediately. It takes time to talk about and work through what an addiction entails and the things each person endured.

In both areas (the person who was addicted and the person trying to help), *be patient.* Be patient with the process of admission and recovery. Be patient as you watch their "reacclimation" into society, church, family, life.

Know that Satan will be at work in both your lives, deceiving you about how long this process should or should not take. Be aware he will place temptations of all kinds in front of you to make you impatient, angry, frustrated, bitter, jealous, and so on. Both parties must be aware of their own propensities for sin and failure. Where you may not be struggling with addiction, you may be judgmental or unkind with your words. You may not have a body image struggle, but you have control and anger issues.

Wherever your journey takes you, let the word of the God guide you.

"Let the word of Christ dwell in you richly, teaching and admonishing one another" (Colossians 3:16).

"Keep watch on yourself, lest you too be tempted. Bear one another's burdens, and so fulfill the law of Christ. For if anyone thinks he is something, when he is nothing, he deceives himself. But, let each one test his own work" (Galatians 6: 1–4).

"Let no corrupting talk come out of your mouths, but only such as is good for building up, as fits the occasion, that it may give grace to those who hear. And do not grieve the Holy Spirit of God, by whom you were sealed for the day of redemption. Let all bitterness and wrath and anger and clamor and slander be put away from you with all malice. Be kind to one another, tenderhearted, forgiving one another, as God in Christ forgave you" (Ephesians 4: 29–32).

Think about It:

What habits can you develop so you can start changing your thinking?

How can you make others aware of your struggles and your desires for change?

In what ways can you be a help to someone struggling with addictive behaviors? Are you doing those things? Why or why not?

Is the Bible a regular part of your interaction with others? Why or why not?

How can having Scripture readily available help you respond biblically to someone struggling with addiction?

If you are the one struggling with an addiction, how can the Word of God help you?

Write a prayer asking God to give you wisdom and to be open to the Spirit's change in your heart, whether you are overcoming addiction or helping bring change to an addictive person's heart.

Preparing for Another Climb

Precious Lord, take my hand;
Lead me on; help me stand.
I am tired; I am weak; I am worn.
Through the storms, through the night,
Lead me on to the light.
Take my hand, Precious Lord—
Lead me on.

—"Precious Lord, Take My Hand"
by Thomas Dorsey

Addiction is just one mountain I have climbed. I am writing about this mountain all while climbing another mountain of mothering small children and navigating the trails and passes of motherhood and parenting. And then, there's being a wife. And a daughter, sister, employee, friend. Life marches on, swiftly and surely. The mountains do not fade until I reach the end of the range.

I can tell you one thing: I am not leaving behind my most valuable resource: my Bible. I am prepared to ask for help and to gain much wisdom from people who have climbed this mountain ahead of me. However, I also recognize my climb will not be the same as anyone else's trek. I am different from everyone else, and my children are not anyone else's children. So in climbing this mountain, I understand that I must continue to be alert for the dangerous side trails and precipices.

How can I (and you!) move on to the next mountain without becoming discouraged or feeling utterly defeated (again)? Or how can I climb this, and other trails, without thinking I will fail (again)?

The Bible makes it clear we, as Christians, are involved in a spiritual war. This war has been raging here on earth since Adam and Eve first sinned. Satan is allowed to deceive, to tempt, to put his powers at work to make us ineffective, unfaithful, and undedicated followers of Jesus. In the book of Ephesians, the Apostle Paul writes of the stark reality of a violent and devastating invisible war.

He declares, "For we do not wrestle against flesh and blood but against the rulers, against the authorities, against the cosmic powers over this present darkness, against the spiritual forces of evil in the heavenly places. Therefore, take up the whole armor of God, that you may be able to withstand in the evil day, and having done all, to stand firm" (Ephesians 6:12–13). He further elaborates on the types of armor to wear as defense against Satan's attacks.

Understanding that I exist in a constant battle made me aware that so much of what I thought was just "life" or "me" or "poor circumstances" are *actually* the schemes of the devil. As I mentioned previously, Satan capitalized on the pride of my heart. He tempted me to believe the things I did and said (under the guise of being a "fine" Christian girl) were actually *mine* to claim as my own righteousness. He subtly planted seeds of deceit and unbelief about who God is, who I am in relation to Him, and how that relationship should affect everyone else.

Satan is real. The battle is real. The trails are treacherous. And the climb dangerous. And now that I have an awareness of this fact, I dare not climb any more mountains without looking out for his traps. And neither should you.

The important part of this is realizing your areas of weakness and struggle. If, as a Christian, you do not know the sins you are consistently prone to committing, Satan has you right where he wants you. In that place of naïve comfort, you set yourself up to become apathetic, deceived, and ineffective. Being unaware of the daily attack on your soul allows for the back door to be opened and the enemy to slip right in, unnoticed.

I must be aware of how I think. When I see that woman eating so much (and she is still skinny and attractive), I must remember that my body is not my own. I have been bought by the blood of Jesus, so

I must not think that I deserve what she has. I have the righteousness of Christ; therefore, I should not be dwelling on the temporal appeal or look of a physical body.

I must be aware of how I respond. I should not respond to a comment about someone "feeling fat" or "needing to go on a diet" with sarcasm or negativity. Instead, I must encourage them in Christ, all while reminding myself that God has called us to be holy in all our conversations.

I should not be someone who tears others down with my speech or my thinking. This is *hard*. The devil so easily wants to convince me that I deserve to look a certain way or that I am not nearly as "bad" or as much of a "basket case" as so-and-so. He loves to get me to dwell on the past and my mistakes and sins. He loves to place in my path circumstances and responses out of my control to get me to respond in anger or impatience. He loves when I respond with a judgmental or negative attitude toward the sins of someone else.

All these things happen subtly. Perhaps someone has approached you about the way you speak to others or the way you constantly express worry and doubt. Maybe you lie consistently. Maybe you easily respond with anger. Maybe you regularly demonstrate impatience. Maybe you consistently berate others (with either your words or thoughts).

All these things are sin. All these are subtle attacks of the devil to convince you about what you "deserve" or how you should or should not be treated. For example, I find myself becoming easily angered or impatient with my kids. I *know* these are attacks from the devil. So how can I respond rightly instead of taking those little side trails or stumbling onto that control trail again?

Constant practice. Constant awareness of sin. And in that moment of sin, confession. Immediate confession.

After Paul writes about the full armor of God to wear, he instructs the believers to "[pray] at all times in the Spirit, with all prayer and supplication. To that end keep alert with all perseverance" (Ephesians 6:18). Daily sin is a reality. You *must* be alert. This requires constant communication with God. When Paul says, "Pray at all time," he means exactly that! In the moments of spiritual attack, you dare not communicate on your own terms with the enemy.

Communicating with God takes effort. Prayer takes discipline. I have found, though, when I get caught up in the everyday conflicts without communicating with God, my responses and methods of warfare lead to ditched efforts and manifold frustrations.

Praying at all times does not mean sitting in your closet and praying all day. We all have lives and responsibilities to perform. So in order to maintain that communication during our daily battles, our furtive, focused, minute-by-minute prayers can be described as "darts" going out against the enemy.

In those moments we fail to seek God's guidance and help, He promises to forgive us and to help us when our words and efforts fall short of His glory. This is *war*! How prepared are you to face your foe?

Think about It:

Are you aware of your sin daily? Why or why not?

When you are confronted (whether by the Holy Spirit or by another person), how do you respond?

Does your response indicate a desire to forsake sin? Why or why not?

Do you readily confess sin as it is brought to your attention?

How aware are you of the spiritual battle raging around you?

Ask God to make you aware of the daily battles Satan is fighting against you. Ask Him to reveal areas where you need greater strengthening to fight against his schemes.

The Goal—"Take 2"

Forbid it, Lord, that I should boast
Save in the death of Christ my God
All the vain things that charm me most,
I sacrifice them to His blood.

Were the whole realm of nature mine—
That were a present far too small.
Love so amazing, so divine,
Demands my soul, my life, my all.

—"When I Survey the Wondrous Cross"
by Isaac Watts

Addictions certainly cannot be written off as a "one and done" experience. Whatever your addictive struggle has been, know that the recovery process is long, yet it is *worth* it. However, addictions of all kinds remain lurking around every corner of your heart and mind.

So as you seek to renew your mind, to be aware of your sin, and to confess and fight the battle against the schemes of the devil, you must remember one very important thing: to rely only on Christ.

This may seem an obvious instruction, but this entire journey of addiction began when I continually relied on myself. You can do all the things—read your Bible, confess your sin, memorize Scripture, pray—but until you recognize you "doing" all those things through your own power avails nothing, you will continue to live frustrated and defeated.

I do not wish to discourage you. I have been learning (through much frustration myself) that God does not want me to do all the "right" things. God wants me to know Him. And in order to know Him, I must stop doing all the things "my way."

This requires letting go of religious, prideful expectations. This means setting aside my judgments and opening myself up to honest, painful scrutiny. This involves putting aside my comfortable Christianity and embracing the realities of Spirit-filled living.

In a world that promotes success, money, and "believing in yourself," God has called His children to live as "slaves of [Him]" (Romans 6:22). So what does this mean?

I have mentioned previously how the books of the prophets in the Old Testament helped me grasp the rebellious nature of my heart. And not only did God reveal to us how pride and rebellion reject His nature and plan for us, He also revealed how we should truly live to please Him. In the book of Jeremiah, God says, "Let not the wise man boast in his wisdom, let not the mighty man boast in his might, let not the rich man boast in his riches, but let him who boasts boast in this, that he understands and knows me, that I am the LORD who practices steadfast love, justice, and righteousness in the earth. For in these things I delight" (Jeremiah 9: 23–24).

God does not need you to be smart. God does not need you to be wealthy or successful. God wants you to know Him. He wants you to understand His love for you. He wants you to be aware of His justice and righteousness. He wants you to understand how your sin affects your ability to communicate with Him. He delights in your coming to Him with a humble spirit, recognizing your efforts to be a "good Christian" are futile unless you truly seek His face.

And this means letting go of your control. This means throwing your hands up and saying, "Okay, God, I'm done trying to do it all." This means confessing your sin. This means doing the very things your heart and mind are telling you not to do. Like writing this book. Like admitting I failed. Like being vulnerable. Like communicating honestly.

All the things I struggle against—admitting failure, being honest about my sin, letting go of control—are the very things God has revealed to be the barriers in my ability to know Him.

In the book of Philippians, Paul writes about how he was "it" when it came to religious success. He had all the credentials of a good follower of God. However, he emphatically declares those things were complete loss compared with knowing Christ. In fact, he goes so far as to equate all that "good stuff" he was doing for God as trash (Philippians 3:7–8)! How could he say this? Paul could only say this because he recognized who God really is. He recognized God is not concerned with how many times we have read the entire Bible. God is not concerned with how many church services we have attended. God does not need us to say or even do all the right things. No, Paul could say these things (and we can too!) when he realized truly knowing Christ surpasses all the "stuff."

Paul elaborates this idea by declaring his goal is to "know [Christ] and the power of his resurrection... [to] share his sufferings, becoming like him in his death, that by any means possible I may attain the resurrection from the dead" (Philippians 3:10–11). You may be thinking, *How is that possible? Look at how I have messed things up already. I can't really "know" God, can I?*

Yes, you can. And yes, I can too! Thankfully, Paul encourages us that the goal of knowing Christ is not something magically granted or specially gifted. No, knowing Christ involves a constant, consistent effort, completely dependent on the work of Christ. Paul says, "Not that I have already obtained this [knowing Christ) or am already perfect, but I press on to make it my own. Brothers, I do not consider that I have made it my own. But one thing I do: forgetting what lies behind and straining forward to what lies ahead" (Philippians 3:12–13).

Let's pause a minute here. In knowing Christ, Paul says we are to "forget what lies behind." This is hard. That addiction that has so ruled your life and my life—we are supposed to forget about that. (That's not to say we pretend it never happened. No, that means we are not supposed to be defined by it anymore!) So in my case, I must forget that anorexia defined me. I am *not* defined by being skinny or beautiful or religiously "good." I am defined by the righteousness I have in Christ (Philippians 3:9). Do you know this, dear believer? You are not defined by the good things you are doing. You are defined by the righteousness of Christ! You cannot and could not become righteous of your own accord. *He* already paid it all for you. Stop living as though you need to add to His righteousness.

Furthermore, as you remember His righteousness and forget your own fumbling attempts, you strain forward to what lies ahead for you. And what is that exactly? We strain forward to "the prize for the upward call of God in Christ Jesus" (Philippians 3:14). What does that mean? What is the prize? The prize is becoming like Christ. And while Scripture makes it clear we will never fully become like Christ in our earthly state, the goal is that. The goal is the glories of heaven and reveling in the divine perfection of our eternal home.

Is that your goal? In your everyday struggles, can you say, "My goal is being like Christ?" This includes, as Paul says, "shar[ing] his sufferings, becoming like him in his death." How humiliating the cross was for Jesus! How incredibly "beneath Him" is our lowly estate! And yet, He chose to come as a baby to this mean, disgusting earth. He, who divinely created all things, lived among those sin-cursed beings to be despised and rejected by them. He who patiently and lovingly healed the sick and taught truth, then willingly endured the shame and pain of the cross and succumbed to death. And can you, believer, truly say you want to become like Him?

Oh, how glorious the thought to then consider death was not the end for Christ! For though He died, death could not hold Him fast! In full control of His divinity, He broke the curse of sin and death, crushing Satan's power and providing the blessed eternity of holy heaven to all who will believe in His name! And that means you and me—we who have called upon His name for salvation have this hope! We have this goal to enjoy the bliss of heaven with Him who has gone before us. *Jesus.* The Author and Perfecter of our faith. So as we reconsider our goal, consider the author of that goal. Christ has left us His example. He has given us all the things we need to become like Him. We must stop trying to reinvent Jesus. Instead, we ask Him to reinvent us. Ask Him to change your heart and your goals. Ask Him to help you truly *know Him.* Set aside the notions and preconceived ideas of who you "think" Jesus is, and truly get to know Him. Seek to understand Him. He *delights* in that goal.

Paul beautifully concludes this lofty declaration with a reminder: "But our citizenship is in heaven, and from it we await a Savior, the Lord Jesus Christ, who will transform our lowly body to be like his glorious body, by the power that enables him even to subject all things to himself. Therefore, my brothers, whom I love and long for, my joy and crown, stand firm thus in the Lord, my beloved" (Philippians 3:20–21, 4:1).

Let's change our goals, beloved. Let's finish climbing our mountain ranges with greater wisdom and stronger faith and by becoming more like Christ. For one day, we shall see Him face-to-face, and may we not be ashamed at that meeting! Know Him. Understand Him. Delight in Him.

For the glory of the Lord! Amen and amen!

Think about It:

How have you tried to please God by adding your own righteousness?

Does knowing Christ in His sufferings and even perhaps in His death scare you? Why?

In what ways have you limited knowing God?

Are you afraid to become like Christ? Why?

How does having an eternal perspective change the way you define your "life goals"?

Write a prayer asking God to change your goals. Ask Him to help you forget the things behind you and to strain forward toward the prize of becoming like Christ!

In the Everyday Passes

I need Thee ev'ry hour, most gracious Lord;
No tender voice like Thine can peace afford.
I need, Thee, O, I need Thee—
Ev'ry hour I need Thee.
O bless me now my Savior—
I come to Thee!

—"I Need Thee Ev'ry Hour" by Annie S.
Hawks and Robert F. Lowry

I want to share a few things that have helped me in everyday situations. Let's face it—the everyday stuff of life is where the true tests lie regarding overcoming addiction. In the quiet moments. In the alone moments. In the busy moments.

I have found one of the greatest helps to me in overcoming my desire for control is to serve others. Having children has certainly helped with this! And I have found when I let go of controlling my marriage and instead *served* my husband, our relationship has become closer and sweeter.

How can you serve? A great way to serve others is to cook for them! This, obviously, goes against the very mantra of an anorexic person, but in many ways, cooking and baking food to give to others has been a huge part of my healing process. Learning to see food as a gift from God to share with others has helped change my perspective.

Look for ways to invest in someone else. In focusing so much on our addiction, you and I have been living to please ourselves. A huge part of overcoming that addiction, then, is living, first and foremost, to please God. In order to please and love Him, we are called to love others. And loving others can look like a lot of different things, but it always involves letting go of your control. Let go of your control to look a certain way before others; instead, ask yourself what would be helpful and would show God's love to that other person. If you have a person you are accountable with/to, try doing something special for them. Write notes. Buy coffee. Make a gift. Give of your time. Watch their kids or pet. Start doing things for others—things you previously said you would never do! Watch how God uses those things to increase your love for Him and others.

In the everyday food struggle, I have found it takes baby steps. As an anorexic person, I am going to assume you may have been previously teased or made to feel inferior for your weight or appearance. Now, as you try to move on from those memories as well as the control of your body, it's hard to know what and how to eat again. Often, the struggle lies with wanting to enjoy food again, but enjoying and indulging in things like you did as a kid will probably make you unhealthy/fat again. So how do you embrace food again without freaking out and panicking about it all over again?

Let me say, it takes time, and I am still learning. Certainly, we all want to eat healthy. We don't need to (nor should we) eat junk food all the time. Find a balance. Enjoy the good things. Take extra helpings of the vegetables and fruits. It may feel adventurous to enjoy a sandwich/wrap or to eat meat again. Whatever it was you were denying yourself, eat (and enjoy!) that item. For me, I had this aversion to eating any bread. Now, I make our own bread and usually eat one or two pieces every day. If you can or find it helpful, meet with a nutritionist to discuss what foods and menus would help you find a new balance to eating properly.

What about junk food (going out to eat, etc.)? This is a hard one for me. I cringe at the thought of eating a double cheeseburger or indulging in a large fry. So I don't. And you don't have to either. Thankfully, many fast-food places now offer healthier options. So start with that. Be careful to not let your desires for control or anger at others dictate your choices or responses to these situations. Ask God to help you respond with wisdom and patience.

Comments and criticisms from other people often lead to discouragement for an anorexic person. Even if the person making the comments has no clue you have struggled with anorexia, the comments about "so-and-so being fat" or "how they need to go on a diet" can be fuel to a struggling and confused heart and mind.

In situations like this, sometimes it helps to actually say something and honestly (yet lovingly) point out that discussing a person's weight (especially behind their back!) is not kind, nor is it pleasing to God. Additionally, someone consistently talking about how they need to lose weight or go on a diet can be an indication that person struggles with body image also and is looking for affirmation or support from others. Ask God to help you respond with grace, love, and honesty.

In the right situation, sharing your own struggles can be an eye-opener for an otherwise oblivious person. Many people have no idea the struggles and pull of anorexia (or any addiction). And in respect to that, they have no comprehension of the ongoing efforts to overcome that addiction.

In all of life, you must remember to let the Spirit of God be your guide. In the everyday situations and struggles, recognize God will give you grace and strength. He will grant you wisdom and discernment. And when you fail, He will give you help to continue to learn and conquer the foes shooting darts into your mind and heart.

Come to Him, every day, looking for His help, His enabling, and His wisdom. You cannot climb down that mountain and make it through the passes of your mountain range on your own. Remember to look at the right map. Ask for help from the people who have faithfully gone before you.

We can overcome, in the power of His might!

About the Author

Amanda Reed is a wife and mom, currently residing in New England. You can contact her and read more about God's work in her life at amandareed.org. *Sometimes It Takes a Mountain* is her first book.